Original title:
Squid and the Stars

Copyright © 2025 Creative Arts Management OÜ
All rights reserved.

Author: Vivian Laurent
ISBN HARDBACK: 978-1-80587-260-3
ISBN PAPERBACK: 978-1-80587-730-1

The Abyssal Canvas

In the depths where monsters grin,
A paintbrush twirls with a fishy fin.
An octopus with colors bright,
Mimics krill in a wobbly flight.

With every stroke a gurgling sound,
As jellyfish float all around.
The reef says, "What a sight to see!"
As clams break dance in harmony.

Nebulae and Nematocysts

A comet swirls, a bubble too,
With tentacles that dance and skew.
In cosmic frolics, they play tag,
While starfish cheer and clams all brag.

The cosmic soup is thick and funny,
As creatures laugh, it's wild and sunny.
With eyes so big, they whirl and spin,
In the swirling cosmos, they dive right in.

Phosphorescent Dreams

In a glow of blues and glowing greens,
The critters plot their sneaky schemes.
They twirl on currents, jolly as can be,
In phosphorescent waves, they wiggle with glee.

A fishy joke ignites the crowd,
As bubbles burst and laughter loud.
"Did you hear?", a fish doth beam,
"The universe laughs in a bubble's gleam!"

Nautical Nebulas

With fins that flutter like a tease,
The cloud of fish swim with such ease.
Through galactic waves, they twist in time,
A cosmic ballet, oh so sublime!

A crab dons shades, strutting his style,
As cosmic waves make all things worthwhile.
They dance on tides, all wild and free,
Giggles echo in the salty sea.

Odyssey through Celestial Waters

A goofy creature with eight flailing limbs,
Dances through bubbles, doesn't care for whims.
Waving at planets, a joyful parade,
Each wink at a comet, makes laughter cascade.

Wearing a helmet made of bright moon cheese,
Chasing the stardust, with effortless ease.
He spins 'round a galaxy, what a madcap,
Swirling and twirling in an astral flap!

Shadows in the Milky Tide

In the night tide, a shadow does scoff,
Tickling the dark until it bursts off.
With a wink and a wiggle, it plays peek-a-boo,
Turning the silence into chuckles anew.

Flipping through waves, it tells silly tales,
Of space jellybeans and near-miss whale trails.
Array of odd friends, a crew of delight,
They splash through the cosmos, giggling at night!

Mysteries of the Deep Blue Sky

In depths of the cosmic, where giggles reside,
A creature unravels the fun on the ride.
With a twist of its tentacle, it writes notes,
On the backs of lost meteors, wearing bright coats.

They stumble through galaxies, bursting with glee,
Singing off-key to the tune of the sea.
Each splash of adventure paints laughter in void,
Mysteries laugh, with secrets enjoyed!

Astral Symphony of the Abyss

A jester in darkness, with lights on its face,
Composes a symphony, a cosmic embrace.
With violin stars and a harp made of void,
It dances through echoes, joyfully buoyed.

The planets all giggle, as notes swirl around,
A melody bouncing from sky to the ground.
With silly little hops and a luminescent grin,
This creature's delight is where laughter begins!

Dreaming in Ink

In the depths where ink flows wide,
Creatures play and dance with pride.
They twirl around in colors bright,
Painting dreams in the soft moonlight.

A laughing crab shimmies with glee,
While fish debate what could it be.
A jellyfish jigs with a wink,
Sipping on bubbles, it starts to think.

A dolphin flips in a sparkling splash,
As octopuses put on a bash.
They write their tales in swirling lines,
Underwater parties, where everyone shines!

So here beneath the surface deep,
The underwater secrets keep.
With every giggle and every cheer,
These inked stories bring us near!

Heartbeats Beneath the Waves

Beneath the waves, where laughter swells,
A sea of giggles, where fun dwells.
The crab sings songs of silly styles,
While starfish hold hands and strike some smiles.

A turtle with glasses reads a book,
While fish gather 'round for a story nook.
They share wild tales of fishy pranks,
And how the seaweed shimmies in colorful ranks.

A whale blows bubbles, a fountain of fun,
While seahorses race, oh what a run!
They tickle the currents, joyous and free,
With heartbeats echoing, such harmony!

So let's dive deep with a splash and a whirl,
In this watery world, let laughter unfurl.
With echoes of joy cascading all day,
In the ocean's heart, we'll dance and play!

The Ocean's Constellation

Look up high, see the shimmering glow,
Fish in formation, putting on a show.
They twinkle and wink, like stars at night,
Creating patterns that bring delight.

A clownfish juggles seaweed and shells,
While anemones giggle, casting their spells.
The angelfish dances in polka dots bright,
The ocean's own lights, a whimsical sight.

A coral reef band starts to jam,
With trumpet fish playing a funky slam.
Turtles tap-dance, flaunting their flair,
As bubbles burst into giggles in the air!

So let's find joy in this watery maze,
Where laughter and wonder set hearts ablaze.
In this vast deep, let us celebrate,
The ocean's wonders that never abate!

Celestial Symphony

In the depths where laughter intertwines,
A symphony plays, with funky designs.
Musical waves, they swirl and spin,
With rhythm and fun, let's all dive in.

The seaweed sways to a catchy beat,
While conga line crabs tap their feet.
A playful dolphin leads the dance,
Inviting all fish to join in a prance!

The jellyfish glide in a wavy delight,
Creating a disco of colors so bright.
With sparkling bubbles that float all around,
The ocean's own music, a joy to be found.

So join the chorus of chuckles and glee,
In this world of dreams beneath the sea.
With tunes that bounce like waves in the air,
A celestial symphony that's beyond compare!

Murmurs in the Cosmos

In the deep where squid do glide,
They hold a party, full of pride.
With glowing lights and ink in hand,
They dance around, a merry band.

Crustaceans playing tag with glee,
While starfish try to join the spree.
Octos spin in circles tight,
As jellyfish float, a dazzling sight.

But what's that noise? A comet's call,
It tickles fins and makes them fall.
The echoes bounce through darkened space,
A cosmic giggle in this place.

So join the fun, don't be afraid,
In the ocean's depths, it's all a charade.
With laughter bubbling from the floor,
Across the void, we'll dance and soar.

A Constellation of Arpographs

In underwater galleries so bright,
Creatures sketch with all their might.
Their pencils swirl, and colors fly,
Creating dreams beneath the sky.

With every squiggle, laughter bursts,
As fish join in with silly firsts.
A crab critiques with tiny claws,
While eels pose proudly, giving pause.

Don't let the rocks be too mundane,
Add a doodle of a fish in rain.
The artistic vibes are quite distinct,
As bubbles pop and colors linked.

A masterpiece beneath the waves,
Where playful art and fun behaves.
Each stroke, a gleeful tale retold,
In a gallery where dreams unfold.

The Luminous Abyss

In a realm where light does twirl,
Anemones dance with a playful whirl.
They giggle softly as they sway,
In currents where the fish hold sway.

With glowing orbs like bright balloons,
The sea creatures sing to mystic tunes.
A clownfish jests, a silly jest,
While seahorses take a cozy rest.

Octopus jester, arm-spread wide,
Tells a tale of cosmic ride.
With ink and bubbles, laughs arise,
In this abyss, fun never dies.

So come join the underwater mirth,
Where laughter echoes, it's a birth.
A party lies beneath the foam,
Where every creature feels at home.

Echoes from the Twilight

In the twilight, where the shadows play,
Creatures giggle in a playful array.
A lanternfish hums a quirky tune,
While grinning snails dance by the moon.

With laughter bouncing off the stones,
The seafloor echoes silly tones.
A group of crabs, they all unite,
In ticklish games till morning light.

In tides that swirl, their joy is clear,
As stingrays glide and gently steer.
They laugh at currents, give them chase,
What a joy to share this space!

So swim along, don't be too shy,
Join in the fun as time drifts by.
In twilight's charm, we'll lose the stress,
Amid the waves, we'll all express!

Creatures of Cosmic Depth

In the deep where the bubbles rise,
Dancing fish wear comical ties.
Jellybeans float with a giggling sound,
While the grinning eels twist all around.

A turtle plays chess with a whale so grand,
While tiny shrimp form a marching band.
The water's a party, oh what a scene,
With seaweed confetti and jellybean cuisine!

A crab throws its claws up in laughter,
As octopi juggle, a wacky disaster.
Bubbles are bursting with bubbles of glee,
In this oceanic circus, so wild and free!

Luminous Abyssal Ballet

The dancers prance on the ocean floor,
With glittering fins that twinkle and soar.
A sea lion spins in a sequined beret,
While the snails do the cha-cha in a slow ballet.

Starfish applaud with their wiggly arms,
While seahorses whisper their secret charms.
The clownfish chuckle, all painted in hue,
As they twirl around like a wacky revue.

Anemones sway with a swishy delight,
As they bask in the glow of the underwater light.
When the curtains of algae rise high and wide,
The ocean's a stage, come enjoy the ride!

Echoes of the Cosmic Ocean

In the depths where weird echoes play,
Bubbly sounds hijinks on display.
A dolphin giggles, tickling the tide,
While an octopus jokes, filled with pride.

Bubbles arise, creating a tune,
As fish disco dance beneath the moon.
With every splash that ripples the sea,
Comedic chaos, wild and free!

Urchins act silly, spouting sweet rhymes,
They crack corny jokes, oh my, how it chimes!
The humor of waves that laps at the shore,
Is a laughter-filled feast, always wanting more!

The Inked Path between Worlds

A busy ink cloud moves through the blue,
Trail of giggles, slippery and true.
With squishy inhabitants, full of delight,
Every twist and turn brings a new sight.

An ink-slinger crafts a riddle or two,
As wiggly creatures join in the crew.
The path that they trace, a comedy pure,
With every funny jiggle, you can't help but lure.

Beneath the waves, a quirky parade,
With tentacles waving, an ink-splashed charade.
The echoes of laughter that softly resound,
As friendships are inked and joy knows no bound!

Currents of Starlight

In the sea where fish wear hats,
And jellyfish dance like acrobats,
A creature floats with such great flair,
Its tentacles waving without a care.

It dreams of planets made of cheese,
While nibbling on some ocean peas,
With every swirl and every twist,
It claims the night can't be dismissed.

Bubbles rise with silly sounds,
As laughter echoes, joy abounds,
With glimmering winks, it greets the night,
Spreading laughter in soft moonlight.

So if you hear a giggling tide,
Know beneath the waves it's filled with pride,
A cosmic clown in watery suit,
With starlit jokes that are quite cute.

Beneath the Cosmic Surface

Underneath the shimmering blue,
Creatures giggle and play peek-a-boo,
They tell tales of clouds and suns,
While draping clouds in jelly runs.

With every wave, a chuckle gleams,
In murky waters, bubble dreams,
A playful dance of flips and swirls,
Where even seaweed laughs and twirls.

They sing of worlds where fish wear shoes,
And squirt their ink in vibrant hues,
In this realm of hugs and giggle fits,
Each splash of joy, a punchline hits.

So dive into this joyful sea,
Where every fin holds a mystery,
And beneath the cosmic surface wide,
Life is fun, with stars as guide.

Celestial Dances at Dusk

As the sun dips low and twirls its rays,
Creatures gather for playful displays,
Galactic glee in shimmering light,
Under the waves, it's such a sight.

In this realm of jolly pranks,
Seagrass sways, and laughter clanks,
A constellation mapped in giggles,
As the moon above gently wiggles.

Stars wink with a mischievous glint,
While fish make faces and pop a hint,
It's a ballet wrapped in cosmic cheer,
Where every splash brings a hearty cheer.

So if you see a whirlpool laugh,
Know it's just cosmic mischief on the half,
With creatures jiving wherever they roam,
In the ocean's heart, they're right at home.

Whispers from the Deep

Down in the depths, where shadows play,
Creatures tell tales in a funny way,
With whispers soft beneath the tide,
Where secrets and giggles often bide.

A friendly ray glides by with flair,
Tickling coral without a care,
The octopus winks, dressed up in style,
Chatting away, tickling all the while.

"Hey, did you hear?" whispers the snail,
"The moon once slipped and started to sail!"
Each line brings giggles, wide-eyed delight,
With chuckling currents swirling at night.

So listen close to the jests of the deep,
In each splash and ripple, laughter to keep,
For down in the ocean, in each little groove,
The whispers of joy in waves gently move.

Celestial Cephalopod

In the depths, a wiggly friend,
Swirling arms that twist and bend.
He wears a hat of bright galore,
Sipping stardust by the shore.

With a wink and playful twirl,
He dances in a cosmic swirl.
Tentacles juggling moonlit cheese,
Feeding fish with laughter's breeze.

His jokes, they float on bubbles high,
Tickling the fish that pass him by.
He speaks in giggles, gurgles too,
Making the cosmos laugh anew.

A guardian of the silly waves,
Saving dreams that the ocean saves.
With every splash, he spreads some cheer,
Our funny friend, forever near.

Dance of the Inked Cosmos

Under waves of swirling light,
An octopus prepares for flight.
With each dip and sway, a giggle bursts,
In the party where all things thirst.

His ink trails sparkle, rainbow bright,
Drawing doodles of sheer delight.
While turtles tap their clumsy feet,
The fish all join with flippered beat.

Anemones sway with gleeful glee,
As jellyfish do the cha-cha free.
With every twist, the ocean beams,
In this moonlit ball of watery dreams.

So come one, come all, to the fun parade,
In this ocean of laughter, no one's afraid.
They dance till dawn with bubbles galore,
In the cosmic waltz they all adore.

Ocean's Luminous Dream

In the night, the sea does glow,
A creature with style, steals the show.
Sporting glasses, oh so chic,
He jests and dances, what a freak!

With bioluminescent flair,
He throws a party, everywhere.
Crabs bring snacks, clams serve drinks,
While dolphins join, with playful winks.

A treasure trove of jolly sounds,
Bubbles bursting all around.
In a world where giggles reign,
Even starfish join the fun train!

So dive on in, don't be shy,
Join the shimmering, starry sky.
With a twirling dance, the night's aglow,
In this wondrous dream where laughter flows.

Abyssal Voyage to the Infinite

To the abyss, a merry trip,
Where creatures jest and take a sip.
A kraken laughs with chortles loud,
While critters gather, joyful crowd.

They navigate through currents strong,
Singing sea shanties, loud and long.
With every turn, new friends appear,
The deep blue's full of cheer and cheer.

With a splash and a twirl, they spin with grace,
Creating bubbles, a colorful place.
A fish in a hat, oh what a sight!
In this voyage of delight, all is right.

So raise your glass to the waves we roam,
In this undersea, where laughter's home.
With every fin and every grin,
The journey begins where the fun won't thin.

Celestial Map of the Deep

In the ocean's glow, fish twirl in jest,
They swim like acrobats, never take rest.
With bubbles and giggles, they dance on by,
Mapping the wonders where happy fish fly.

The crabs hold a meeting, with shells all aglow,
They vote on the best way to put on a show.
With a flip and a flap, they try to impress,
As mollusks all laugh, causing quite the mess.

A sea turtle sings, a tune quite absurd,
To the rhythm of coral that's never unheard.
The jellyfish glow, like lights in a spree,
In a world where the sea is so silly and free.

Beneath the blue waves, where the laughter will swell,
Creatures of mischief, oh can't you just tell?
With a wink and a splash, they'll welcome you there,
In a cosmic playground, full of giggles and flair.

Cosmic Ballet

In a realm where the waves do a pirouette,
The fish in tuxedos are ready to bet.
With melodious swirls, the seaweed takes flight,
Dancing along through the blues and the light.

The sardines form lines, all twinkling and bright,
As dolphins perform, their jumps sheer delight.
With flippers so graceful, they twirl and they spin,
Creating a spectacle, everyone wins.

Octopus partners can't follow the beat,
Tripping on tentacles, oh what a feat!
While starfish applaud with their arms all the way,
The show must go on, come what may.

Rays slide on in, just in time for the fun,
With a wink of their eyes, the ballet's begun.
In this watery stage, where the humor runs deep,
Every creature's welcome to join in and leap.

The Starlit Depths

In the darkness below where the funny fish roam,
They tell tall tales, making laughter their home.
With glow-in-the-dark smiles, they shine like the night,
Creating a spectacle, oh what a sight!

A playful sea horse rides bubbles like a wave,
While clowns in the current are all being brave.
Fish in a frenzy, parade all around,
In the starlit abyss, pure joy can be found.

The angler's bright light is a flicker of glee,
Attracting the giggles from all in the sea.
With plankton confetti falling down in a flurry,
They dance like it's nothing, no need to worry.

As the moon lights the water with shimmering grace,
Creatures of humor delight in the space.
In the depths of the ocean, where folly does creep,
All dive in for laughter, in waves oh so deep.

Wonders of the Tidal Wave

The tide rolls in, with a splash and a cheer,
Creatures are laughing, there's nothing to fear.
With a wink of the whale and a twist of the crab,
The whole ocean's party, it's quite a fab tab.

Seagulls are swooping, sharing fishy delights,
As barnacles chuckle on breezy sea heights.
The oysters clap shells, in rhythm they sway,
To the frothy old tune of the ocean's ballet.

Playful as dolphins, making waves of their own,
They leap and they dive, in joy they have grown.
With laughter as currency and bubbles as gold,
The wonders of water are truly behold!.

So gather your friends to this watery stage,
Where laughter and antics can never age.
In the wonderful whirl where the tides dance and play,
It's a splashy-filled journey, come join the parade!

Ocean's Whisper

In the deep, where fish do wiggle,
A cephalopod loves to giggle.
He tickles the crabs with a smile,
Making the jellyfish dance for a while.

With tentacles swirling, he jives,
Tickling the seaweed, it thrives.
Anemones sway to his rhythm,
Laughing and twirling in their prism.

The dolphins join in the fun,
Under the moon and shining sun.
They flip and twist in a grand parade,
While our creature plays serenade.

What lives in these depths, oh so bright,
A jester of ocean, a pure delight.
Each splash and giggle echoes wide,
Underwater antics, a joyous ride.

Celestial Depths

In the midnight blue, things get silly,
A creature with arms, oh what a dilly!
He dons a hat made of coral and shells,
And plays peek-a-boo where the deep-sea dwells.

Stars twinkle above, but he's got his own flair,
Swaying to rhythms of an underwater air.
With each little dance, he sends bubbles anew,
Leaving fish giggling, it's the best kind of view.

He tries to send messages up to the moon,
But they get lost in a very big tune.
With laughter echoing through waves of delight,
Who knew the sea could be this bright?

Amidst the dark, he shines like a flame,
In this watery circus, no two days the same.
As wave after wave carries giggles away,
He keeps us all laughing, come join in the play!

Celestial Cephalopod

In a galaxy where sea creatures lie,
A funny fellow reaches for the sky.
With goofy eyes and a wobbly flair,
He's searching for snacks in the currents, beware!

He drifts through the currents, swirling about,
And stirs up a ruckus, there's never a doubt.
With a bubble for a hat and a laugh that erupts,
He makes all the fishes feel happy and pumped!

Exploring the depths with a tickle or two,
He plays hide and seek in the midnight blue.
The anemones giggle, the clams try to dance,
While our splendid cephalopod goes into a trance.

His antics keep everyone smiling away,
With tentacles flapping, he steals the show-play.
Though the ocean is vast, in laughter he'll thrive,
In the swirling expanse, he'll always arrive!

Starlit Swirls

Oh what a night in the briny deep,
Where a curious creature stirs from his sleep.
With tentacles stretched in a twinkling dance,
He invites all the fish to join in the prance.

The moon glimmers down, as the bubbles rise,
Our jester in water wears a look of surprise.
He scoops up the stars in a net made of sea,
And giggles with joy, what a sight to see!

With a squish and a squirm, he paints the ocean,
Bright colors swirling cause waves of commotion.
He juggles the seashells, spins seaweed like gold,
While fish whistle tunes that never get old.

In this wondrous realm where laughter does flow,
Every swirl he creates is a marvelous show.
For in the heart of the deep, what a thrill!
Is a charming, funny fellow with endless goodwill!

Whispers of the Tides

In the ocean's bubbly sway,
Dancing creatures play all day.
Tentacles waving, what a sight!
Giggles echo through the night.

Bubbling laughter fills the deep,
Where fish make promises they keep.
With winks and squirts, they scheme so bold,
Tickling bubbles, a jest untold.

An octopus in a tiny hat,
Sips on jelly, what do you chat?
He jokes of sailors lost from sight,
And moonbeams that tickle the night.

As the tide sings its merry tune,
Jellybeans dance under the moon.
Join the party, don't be shy,
Giggle along as the waves sigh.

Enigma of the Abyss

Beneath the waves, what do we find?
A riddle wrapped, oh so unkind.
Strange shadows prance and tease our sight,
Ticklish whispers spin through the night.

Kraken's jokes from the deep sea floor,
Hide under rocks, oh what a bore!
Tentacles twirl like a dancing fool,
Inking secrets, the ocean's rule.

The mermen swim in sparkling glee,
With polished shells, they sing for me.
Their laughter echoes, a bubbling spree,
Enigmas of the deep, wild and free.

Giggling guppies play hide and seek,
In the shadows, they play unique.
What mysteries dwell in the dark below?
Who knows, it's all part of the show!

Glimmers of Starlight

In midnight waters, a gleam appears,
With bubbly laughter and silly cheers.
Shimmering fish in sequined scales,
Tell tall tales of whimsical trails.

The splash of a fin, a burst of fun,
Chasing the beams where the sea meets sun.
Crabs in top hats tap dance and prance,
In this glowing realm of a fishy romance.

A whale makes jokes, rumbles so grand,
While sea turtles groove to the band.
All creatures bask in celestial light,
Painting the waves in laughter bright.

Under the waves, dreams do ignite,
Where jellyfish glow, oh what a sight!
Join in the dance, let your spirits soar,
In the ocean's embrace, forever explore.

Night's Tentacled Embrace

When twilight falls, the sea's alive,
With mischief brewing, the creatures thrive.
Tentacles wiggle in currents free,
As they whisper secrets, just for me.

An octopus with a grand top hat,
Plans shenanigans—imagine that!
He juggles pearls in a playful game,
While shouting out each partner's name.

Lobsters play cards and chefs they tease,
As currents swirl with a splash of ease.
A shark in glasses tries to read,
The menu's hidden in algae weed.

With laughter shared in the moonlit sea,
All creatures dance wild and carelessly.
In night's embrace, where fun prevails,
Join in this frolic, where joy regales.

The Harmonies of the Deep Ocean

In the depths where fish do sing,
A tentacled friend dons a bling.
He twirls and swirls with such delight,
Twirling bubbles, a silly sight.

His antics make the clams all giggle,
As jellyfish dance and wiggle.
They hold a show beneath the tide,
With seaweed fans spread wide and wide.

The crabs clap claws, the shrimp all cheer,
For every belly flop they hear.
With laughter rippling through the sea,
Who knew deep blue could be so free?

A concert filled with fins and shells,
As laughter echoes like the bells.
So here's to the joy in ocean's keep,
Where even the deep can laugh and leap.

Dances Under the Moonlight

When moonbeams kiss the ocean's face,
Creatures come to join the race.
In bubble gowns and clownish glee,
They shimmy in their watery spree.

A playful flounder trips in style,
While seahorses prance a crooked mile.
They twirl and roll, so wild and bright,
With bioluminescent lights in sight.

The oysters snap their shells in time,
As laughter rings with every rhyme.
The starfish groove with wobbly flair,
Making moonlit magic in salty air.

So let the dance beneath the tide,
Bring forth the joy that can't subside.
For every splash holds life's sweet thrill,
A funny tune? Yes, what a skill!

Surfacing Stardust

From ocean's deep to skies above,
A funny friend—a crystal dove.
He jumps and flips in sandy plains,
Leaving behind glittering grains.

With playful puffs, he takes to flight,
Through waves of joy and pure delight.
The twilight sparkles, laughter flows,
As wiggly pals join in the show.

A spinning whirl of glee unfolds,
As creature tales and magic molds.
The night is young, let frolic reign,
For every splash is joy's sweet gain.

So here's to the depths and skies in bloom,
Where funny friends dispel the gloom.
Each twist and turn, a shining jest,
In ocean's heart, we find our rest.

The Deep Sea Dance

Beneath the waves, they glide and sway,
With silly moves, they steal the day.
Tentacles twirl like spaghetti strands,
While fish all giggle from coral lands.

A jellyfish joins, a buoyant friend,
Bopping around as if to pretend.
They bounce and whirl in the ocean's blue,
Creating a party, just for a few.

The crab brings snacks on a tiny tray,
With seaweed chips, they munch and play.
All join in chorus, a giddy tune,
Beneath the glow of a friendly moon.

So join the fun in this underwater spree,
Where laughter bubbles, wild and free.
In deep sea revelry, they unite,
A merry dance 'neath the soft starlight.

Inked Nightfall

Inky shadows spread across the tide,
Creatures caper, nothing to hide.
They chuckle as they paint the sea,
With doodles and squiggles, wild and free.

A pufferfish dons a quirky hat,
While octopuses dance, imagine that!
They squirt their colors, bright and bold,
As the ocean's stories begin to unfold.

With a wave from a fish, the party ignites,
Splashes of laughter, oh what delights!
As the moon winks down, they throw a bash,
With bubble machines and a colorful splash.

And in this inked night, they find their groove,
A comical rhythm, a wobbly move.
In the whimsical depths, they all embrace,
Crafting memories in this jolly space.

Luminescent Tentacles

Underneath the waves, they glow with flair,
Tentacles twirling, a magical air.
Like disco balls in the ocean's dance,
A pulsing rhythm, a bright romance.

They tickle the fish with electric beams,
In shimmering hues, they spark wild dreams.
Every flicker is a giggle sent,
In the depths of hilarity, they're content.

The sea anemone strikes a pose,
With a flippy twist, it even glows.
While crabs in tuxedos join the scene,
Making merry, you know what I mean!

So when the night falls, come take a ride,
Through the luminance with joy as your guide.
In this underwater realm, tales come unfurled,
With tentacles shining, oh what a world!

Cosmic Embrace

In the vastness, where balloons drift high,
Creatures huddle and twinkle with glee.
They play cosmic tag with the passing stars,
Gliding 'round in their celestial cars.

A whale in a top hat sings with flair,
While seals crack jokes, giving laughter air.
They spin through the void, in wobbly glee,
Egged on by the moon's soft melody.

Asteroids dance, and meteors race,
Under this galaxy's warm embrace.
With giggles and snickers, the night is bright,
In a festival of fun, what a sight!

So when the cosmos opens wide,
Dive on in, let your spirit glide.
For in this whimsical, silly space,
Joy takes center stage, a cosmic grace.

Starlit Tides

In waters deep where critters play,
A dance of light in a watery ballet.
Jellyfish glow, they twirl and glide,
While fish do the cha-cha, side by side.

An octopus drags a party hat,
He thinks he's cool, we think he's fat.
With bubbles burst and laughter bright,
They spin around in the bubble light.

Seahorses laugh, they can't quite swim,
They ride the waves on a bubble whim.
The tides may shift, the currents roll,
But fun is found in every shoal.

So come join the feast, let's all dive in,
With seaweed snacks and a silly grin.
The ocean's floor, a kooky place,
Where every wave holds a smiling face.

Deep Sea Whispers

In the depths where shadows play,
Fish gossip softly, echoes sway.
"Did you see the crab in shades?"
"Oh yes, he's still in his charades!"

A clownfish jests with a grumpy crab,
"Your face is like an old, worn tab!"
Shimmery friends in a watery night,
Share secrets that shimmer, out of sight.

The starfish struggle to crack a joke,
But their humor sinks, like a sinking boat.
A turtle chuckles, "You tried your best!"
While sea cucumbers just take a rest.

With bubbles and giggles, the ocean spins,
A dance of delight, where laughter begins.
In a world wrapped in silvery gleams,
The deep sea laughs, in all its dreams.

Ethereal Tentacles

An artisan of the deep, so sly,
With waving arms like a grand old spy.
He twirls and coils, a twisty sight,
In the dance of hues, where all is light.

With every grab, he juggles shells,
Telling tales only the ocean dwells.
"Look at me! I'm the best at this!"
While fish roll their eyes, they can't resist.

He flings a pearl, it glints and sparkles,
Turning the waves into giggly sparkles.
The dolphins laugh as they leap high,
"Just don't trip over that very sly guy!"

A theater of antics, a colorful show,
Where the spectacle shines, and friendships grow.
His limbs a flurry, his humor flows,
Under the waves, where the laughter blows.

Galactic Embrace Beneath the Waves

Beneath the foam where laughter swells,
Aliens of the sea cast enchanting spells.
With hugs of bubbles, they float and gleam,
Galactic pals in a wacky dream.

A starry-eyed fish with a wild flair,
Claims to be from the local fair.
"A comet fish, from afar I came,"
While others watch, they can't help but claim.

Squid-like beings wear hats of seaweed,
Claiming fashion tips no one would heed.
They swirl in currents, an elegant group,
With every twist, they form a loop.

So let the waves be a cosmic stage,
For every creature, young and sage.
In a sea of laughter, where dreams ignite,
Galactic buddies dance into the night.

Light at the Ocean's Edge

A fish in a tuxedo danced on the sand,
Sipping seaweed smoothies from a tiny hand.
He invited the crabs for a waltz and a laugh,
Until they all tumbled in a bubbly half.

The moon took a peek from behind a big wave,
Chortling softly at this new seafood rave.
With a splash and a giggle, the party grew loud,
As fish donned their masks to impress the crowd.

Jellyfish juggled pearls with wily grace,
While clams set the table, all ready for space.
With arms full of treasure, they called it a feast,
And danced till the tide claimed their joy as a beast.

Tentacled Reverie

A creature with arms that could wrap 'round the moon,
Sipped bubble tea through a bright pink balloon.
He invited his pals on a wild dance spree,
While a clam played the conch like a goofy MC.

With each twist and twirl, the tide swayed with glee,
Octopuses clapped with eight limbs full of spree.
The sea bed was bouncing with rhythm and cheer,
As fish in bow ties all appeared from the rear.

The sand settled down as they twisted and turned,
With jokes that were salty and laughter that burned.
They knew in this moment, under watery skies,
That fun at the reef could be full of surprise.

Ethereal Currents

In a whirlpool of giggles, a dolphin swirled fast,
Chasing bubbles that shimmered, with joy unsurpassed.
He called to his buddies, "Let's ride the great tide!
We'll surf on the waves with the jellyfish glide!"

The turtles wore helmets, quite stylish and slick,
While seahorses cheered from the driftwood they picked.
With splashes and laughter, they formed a big train,
As the ocean's bright chatter hummed a funny refrain.

They played tag with each current, a slippery race,
Moon beams and laughter all lit up the space.
Each quirk of the sea brought a chuckle or two,
As they danced through the depths, enjoying the view.

Galactic Waters

Under cosmic glow, a whale sang a tune,
With starfish holding mics, a quirky festoon.
The bubbles erupted in laughter and song,
While fish in bright costumes swam proud and so strong.

A comet came down to join in the fun,
Shimm'ring scales and sparkles added to the run.
They bounced on the waves, over moonlit spots,
Turning splash fights into hilarious knots.

With laughter galore, they created a scene,
Where octopus painters made each canvas green.
As star crabs applauded, and bubbles would pop,
This underwater circus just never would stop!

Orion's Inkling

In the depths where ink connects,
A twist of fate, a star perplexed.
With armfuls of squid, oh what a sight,
They scribble poems in the dead of night.

Jokes about lobsters float on by,
As constellations wink from the sky.
A dance with the moon, a splash of ink,
They paint the universe, let us all think.

Each quirk and squirm a cosmic jest,
Tickling the void, a test of zest.
With every giggle from the sea's embrace,
They leave their mark in this silly race.

So wave hello to the glowing fleet,
With ink-stained tentacles, they can't be beat.
In laughter, they drift through cosmic air,
Beneath the glow of a starlit stare.

The Dance of Light and Water

Ripples of giggles in the deep blue,
When creatures collide in a waltz or two.
With flashes of brightness and splashes of fun,
They twirl in a tango, oh what a run!

Light flickers and flutters, like a fleeting sprite,
As waves clink together, they dance with delight.
A pirouette here, a somersault there,
Their laughter resounds in the salty air.

With a wink from a comet and a glow from the sun,
Who knew the ocean could have so much fun?
In this swirling ballet where fish wear their hats,
They giggle and bubble, "We've got this, chaps!"

So come take a plunge, join in the spree,
As giggling stars wink down at the sea.
In rippling waters, the joy won't cease,
Let's dance in the light; may our laughter increase!

Notes from the Celestial Sea

In a cosmic ocean of shimmering glee,
A quirky note floats, "Come dance with me!"
With lyrics of bubbles and rhythms of light,
They serenade laughter under the night.

Each note is a splash, a hint of surprise,
As creatures compose with wonder-filled eyes.
"Do you think the stars get tickled too?"
As they ponder and chuckle, what else can they do?

With octopus gourmets serving ink-filled treats,
They feast on the laughter, not just on the sweets.
A banquet of humor, the seas play along,
While starry-eyed dreamers hum a new song.

So here in the depths, where joy is the key,
Let's jot down the notes from the celestial sea.
With giggles and splashes, let's spread the cheer,
As twinkling companions quickly draw near.

Sculpted by Starlight

In the midnight canvas, a splash, a swirl,
Creatures of whimsy begin to unfurl.
With ink and giggles, they craft their own way,
A masterpiece formed from laughter's ballet.

With tentacles gliding, they mold and they play,
Creating absurdity, night turns to day.
Puppets made of dreams and moonbeams abound,
In this artful world, where joy can be found.

A comet's mischief, a wink from the sun,
With sparkles and splashes, they all join the fun.
Sculpted by starlight, their wishes take form,
In a giggling universe, where oddity's norm.

So step into the art show, where laughter takes flight,
With every creation, the world feels just right.
In this gallery of whimsy, we happily roam,
Together we twinkle, forever at home.

Enigma Beneath the Galactic Veil

In the depths where light's pranked,
A creature danced with style and flank.
With tentacles flailing, it tickled the void,
Creating giggles, delightfully employed.

Stars above chuckled, flickering bright,
As jellyfish jammed joined in the night.
An octopus juggled with playful flair,
While comets swirled in a waltzing air.

Mysterious glimmers tickled its mind,
And echoes of laughter were brightly entwined.
With a wink to the moon, it launched a grand dive,
In the cosmos, the jester took a wild drive.

Galactic giggles echoed so wide,
As space critters gathered, side by side.
Their cosmic capers, a joy to behold,
In this universe, tales of laughter unfold.

Odyssey of Whitecaps and Wonders.

Beneath the waves of azure delight,
A swirl of mischief took playful flight.
With bubbles and foam, it crafted a scene,
Where fish wore hats, quite regal and keen.

A dolphin cracked jokes that echoed with glee,
While seahorses strutted like they were on TV.
The current danced wildly, a waltz with a twist,
As shells told stories that could not be missed.

Anemones chuckled, entwined in the play,
And crabs joined the fun in their own quirky way.
In the ocean's embrace, where laughter prevails,
The wonders of life weave whimsical tales.

From coral confetti to jelly soirée,
Each creature a player in this grand ballet.
With every splash, mischief swam near,
In the kingdom of waves, joy was severe.

Celestial Ink

Across the canvas of midnight ink,
A splash of dreams made the cosmos blink.
With squiggles and swirls of colors aglow,
A whimsical creature set the night in a flow.

It painted its laughter with wiggly strokes,
Creating strange shapes that tickled like jokes.
Galaxies giggled, and planets behaved,
As the quirky artist boldly engraved.

With a brush of the tail, it doodled a sun,
And scribbled to call all the stars for some fun.
While comets crackled in cosmic delight,
The universe chuckled under the light.

So cheers to the jester of heavenly art,
Whose inked laughter plays a bizarre part.
In the tapestry bright, it crafted the cheer,
In this making of worlds, the joy is sincere.

Galactic Tides

In the sway of the moon's mischievous glow,
The tides had a party, putting on a show.
From distant galaxies, wave riders came,
Playing hide-and-seek in the starlit frame.

Waves whispered jokes as they danced on the shore,
While crabs played the drums, wanting more.
A starfish crooned with a voice so absurd,
As tides celebrated with shimmies unheard.

With laughter like foamy bubbles that rise,
The ocean took flight under starlit skies.
Each splish and each splash was a giggly embrace,
As the universe waltzed in sublime space.

So gather your shells and let's join in the spree,
With creatures that tickle the deep briny sea.
In this galactic frolic, where fun has its tides,
Joy flows like currents, as each heart abides.

Whispers of the Deep

In ocean's realm, a dance so bold,
Tall tales of tentacles, fingers of gold.
They giggle at fish, who swim in a rush,
In the depths below, there's always a hush.

A critter with ink, it squirts and it twirls,
Forgetting the time, it swirls and whirls.
The bubbles pop loud, a funny ol' tune,
As creatures groan softly, 'Oh, not this cartoon!'

They hold a debate, in colors so bright,
Who wears the best stripes for a night out of sight?
With chuckles and waves, they fashion a hat,
A top that's just right, a snazzy chit-chat!

But as the tides change, they plan their retreat,
In pockets of laughter, they find their own beat.
So here's to the deep, where nonsense does reign,
Where creatures converse over bubbles and grain.

The Night's Palette

Under the moon, colors start to blend,
Octopus artists, with seaweed to send.
With palettes of shells, and brushes of foam,
They paint in the night, their watery home.

Dancing with jellyfish, waltzing along,
They giggle and splash in a silvery throng.
A fish with a beret, flicking about,
Says, 'Trendy or tacky? I have my doubts!'

With every swirl, a masterpiece grows,
But wait! There's a crab who's stepping on toes!
With pinchers of mischief, he joins in the fun,
While dolphins all laugh, 'Oh, isn't this pun?'

As night drifts away, the art takes its toll,
The water now sparkles like a glittering bowl.
They giggle with glee, beneath rising sun,
In their world under waves, they have so much fun!

Celestial Cuttlefish

Once there was a cuttle, who thought it can fly,
With ink in a bottle, it reached for the sky.
It flicked and it flapped, much to its surprise,
When it landed on clouds, with googly eyes!

'Oh, look at those fish! They're swimming through air!'
Exclaimed the cuttle, twirling without a care.
As gulls passed by, they mocked with a squawk,
'You're out of the water, come here and talk!'

With cosmic confetti falling down for the cheer,
The cuttle made friends, with joy and a sneer.
They danced on the waves, in an aerial race,
In a whirl of delight, without a trace.

But soon it grew tired, and missed the old sea,
'Flying's fine, but the ocean's for me!'
So back to the depths, it paddled with style,
Proclaiming with joy, 'I'll be here a while!'

Veils of the Abyss

In the dark, where secrets twine and grip,
A kraken juggles pearls, sly in its trip.
With eight wobbly arms, it puts on a show,
The audience gasps, then bursts into 'whoa!'

A clam in the back, with humor so dry,
Says, 'Watch how it struggles, just look at it try!'
With quirks and odd tricks, all creatures convene,
A circus of wonders beneath the marine.

'The more that you dive, the funnier it gets!'
Squeals a little shrimp, while sharing its pets.
With a wink and a splash, the act takes a turn,
All jokes from the deep, for laughter we yearn.

And as the night falls, with giggles and play,
The veils of the abyss keep smiles on display.
A world full of jest, where joy knows no bounds,
In the depths of the ocean, true fun resounds!

The Inked Universe

In the dark of the ocean's sway,
A creature chuckles, bright as day.
With a flick of ink, a cosmic dance,
Turns every fish into a twirling prance.

Bubbles giggle, gleeful and round,
As the painted tides swirl all around.
Tentacles wave like a jolly parade,
While the dull fish sit, utterly afraid.

A moonlit giggle in the briny deep,
Where secrets swirl and laughter creeps.
Under seaweed hats and coral ties,
Our inked friend plots in disguise.

In the cosmic tide, laughter flows,
With jellyfish jokes that everyone knows.
So when the waves laugh in the light,
Remember this creature's giggles at night.

Midnight Currents

When night falls in waves of blue,
A prankster whispers, "I'm coming for you!"
With glowing eyes and a cheeky grin,
The currents dance, let the fun begin!

Crabs play tag, shells flying high,
While the little fish can't help but sigh.
"Not again!" they squeak, as they dart away,
From the wild mischief in the ocean's ballet.

The moon winks down on the watery show,
As creatures gather for a late-night glow.
Tails twirl in laughter, waves ripple bright,
The sea's hidden party lasts till daylight.

With flicks and flits, the fun won't cease,
In the deep, there's humor, laughter, and peace.
So come join the currents in the midnight scene,
Where every splash is a joke unforeseen!

Patterns of the Deep

In the depths where the colors swirl,
Lives a jester with a playful twirl.
He paints the ocean with his funny schemes,
In patterns that dance like wild daydreams.

The sea turtles giggle at his ink-stained art,
While starfish chuckle, each playing a part.
"Look at that swirl!" a blowfish will cry,
As a glittering design drifts lazily by.

With a flick and a swish, the ocean's alive,
Creating new laughter in its jester's thrive.
A canvas of fun in bubbles and glee,
Where every ripple brings joy to the sea.

So when you look down at the waves below,
Remember the mishaps that make the tide glow.
Each ink-splash and giggle brings beauty anew,
In patterns of joy that the deep loves to brew.

Celestial Horizons

Up above the briny foam,
Creatures dream of a sparkling dome.
With jellybean stars and candyfish tails,
They race through the ocean with colorful trails.

Dolphins leap, with mischief in mind,
Plotting their pranks, leaving the rest behind.
A manta ray's giggle gets lost in the flow,
While the horizon dances in its radiant glow.

The laughter of fish lights up the sea,
Creating a symphony of glee.
With every flip and a wiggly twirl,
The expanses of joy in waves unfurl.

So let your dreams dive deep with the tide,
Where humor and fun are forever allied.
In horizons celestial, where laughter resides,
Join the ocean's merriment on mischievous rides!

Astral Submersibles

In the depths of night, they dive,
With tentacles waving, they thrive.
Floating in bubbles of light,
What a peculiar sight!

Wobbling around like they own the place,
With jellyfish winks and a smiling face.
They tickle the comets, splash in the dark,
Leaving a trail like a cosmic spark.

Their laughter echoes through the wide expanse,
A dance with the planets, a giggling trance.
Unique are their fancies, absurd their tunes,
Who knew space critters were such loony goons?

So join their madcap interstellar spree,
Where dreams swim freely and joy is key.
In a whirl of color and funky glee,
The universe stirs up a cosmic sea!

Celestial Currents

Rusty old rockets and galactic bays,
They surf on stardust in curious ways.
With a flip and a whirl, they swipe left and right,
Making the Milky Way giggle with delight.

In a current of laughter, they twist and shout,
Who knew cosmic beings could dance about?
They surf on the rings of a smiling old moon,
Riding the waves to a funky new tune.

As meteors zoom, they dodge with a cheer,
Guffaws echo loudly, no need for fear.
Just noodle your arms and let go of the pride,
In these celestial currents, come take a ride!

So let's raise a toast to the best cosmic crew,
For their joy-filled antics, there's always a view.
In the great wide yonder, they frolic and jump,
Creating a whirlpool of giggles and thump!

Ink Blots of Infinity

In the vast expanses where dreams twist and fold,
Are ink blots of infinity gleaming like gold.
With swirls of mischief and splashes of fun,
They bubble and bounce, no need for the sun.

They doodle in space with a cosmic flair,
Creating new worlds to float in the air.
Each blot brings a chuckle, a twirl, and a spin,
With laughter and giggles that shimmer within.

The galaxies peek through with curious eyes,
At these merry scribbles in brilliant disguise.
With twists of the quill and a splash of delight,
They tickle the cosmos all day and all night.

So grab a bright nib and let your thoughts fly,
In the inky expanse, there's no reason to sigh.
For the universe thrives on laughter and fun,
Creating connections where all can be one!

The Cosmic Pool

Dive into the cosmic pool, splash and play,
Where gravity giggles and stars like to sway.
A cannonball into laughter, a float on a beam,
What silly shenanigans this can all seem!

Neptune is juggling, the sun shares a wink,
With playful planets, they dance on the brink.
They swim in the colors of cosmic delight,
Throwing starfish wishes into the night.

Jellyfish drift by with a ticklish grin,
While comets make waves as they zoom and spin.
In this galactic pool of humor and cheer,
The universe's laughter is nothing to fear.

So bring your best jokes and let the fun flow,
As we float on the tides where happiness grows.
In the cosmic pool, let's jump, laugh, and twirl,
A fantastic voyage in a silly swirl!

Quasar and Ink

Inky arms stretch wide and free,
A creature glides, all fancy and spree.
With a wink and a swirl, it paints the sky,
Bright squiggles dancing, oh my oh my!

With each tiny twirl, it giggles a tune,
While cosmic pirates hum under the moon.
The jellies are laughing, they wiggle and sway,
As our inky friend shows them how to play!

Floating through nebulae, painting with glee,
Dodging the comets like it's a spree.
"Catch me if you can!" it bubbles with cheer,
While stardust giggles, from far and near.

Who knew that the cosmos could be so bright,
With an inky dancer of pure delight?
The universe chuckles, a whimsical spree,
As laughter drips down like honey from a tree.

Cosmic Voyage

Off we go, in zany ships,
With jellybeans for snacks and starry sips.
Whirling through the galaxy's bright maze,
Our giggles echo in the cosmic haze.

Aliens wave with tentacled hands,
As we share our jelly plans and bands.
"Have a sip of stardust, it's quite a treat!"
While we bop to their tunes, with cosmic feet.

"Look at that spiral, what a funny dance!"
Twisting through patterns, we leap and prance.
Light years are just a blink, you see,
In this cosmic parade, we are wild and free!

With each twinkle and shimmer, the laughter flows,
On this goofy journey, anything goes!
Stellar adventures in laughter we'll find,
In the cosmic ocean, our dreams unconfined.

Galactic Euphony

Whirly bits here, and squiggly there,
We sing to the meteors flying with flair.
In harmony with lunar light beams,
We create silly songs, woven with dreams.

Each note is a burst of a supernova,
With giggles spinning, like a silly sofa.
Planets sway gently in sync with our glee,
As we serenade comets, wild and free.

Through the Milky Way, our melodies soar,
With echoes and chuckles, forevermore.
"Sing like the asteroids!" we howl with cheer,
As our galactic band brings all far and near.

In an opera of laughter, our spaceships cheer,
With a cosmic concerto that we hold dear.
Together we jive, with each twinkling note,
In the euphony where gags and stardust float.

The Color of Night Ocean

In the deep blue where whispers giggle,
Creatures of whimsy swim and wiggle.
With eyes like saucers, they peek and stare,
At the painted wonders we create with flair.

Waves of laughter ripple through the night,
As playful pranks bring out their delight.
"Look over there, it's a disco ball!"
They wiggle and jiggle, having a ball!

An octopus juggles with a wink and a laugh,
While clams clap their shells, sharing a gaffe.
In this zany ocean where colors collide,
Every splash sends the giggles worldwide!

The corals glow in a spectrum of glee,
With seaweed dancing, oh, wild and free!
The night ocean sparkles with humor and cheer,
As laughter flows freely, bringing all near.

Luminescent Ballad of the Abyss

In the deep where the glowfish play,
A dance of colors, night becomes day.
Tentacles twist in a comical spree,
Chasing bright orbs that giggle with glee.

Bubbles arise with a ticklish sneeze,
As tiny fish dart, doing as they please.
A wobbly creature, quite round and spry,
Tries to hop but just flops, oh my!

Fins flap like flags in a jubilant fray,
Each splash resounds like a warm cabaret.
With jellybeans bouncing, they all shout,
"Who knew the abyss could be so stout?"

So come take a look at this whimsical reef,
Where laughter and humor blend with belief.
For in every corner, a chuckle is found,
In the depths of the sea, joy knows no bound.

Cosmic Currents

Waves shimmer like dreams on a clear, starry night,
With playful skimmers dancing, oh what a sight!
The laughter of bubbles, like children they race,
In this ocean of wonder, there's no time to waste.

A curious critter with a graceful flair,
Tries to wear a hat made of seaweed and air.
It teeters and totters, a sight quite absurd,
While everyone giggles at this 'fashionable' bird.

Swirling around in the milky-blue swirl,
A ticklish sensation, a whirl and a twirl.
With each giggle echoed throughout the vast space,
Joy bounces in currents, setting a pace.

So smile at the antics, let laughter ignite,
In the cosmic dance where the creatures delight.
For every splash carries a hint of surprise,
In this vibrant expanse beneath shimmering skies.

Inked Oracles of the Night

The moonlight drips in ghostly hues,
Where ocean scribes share their quirky news.
Ink pools ripple, as secrets take flight,
In the depths of the ocean, a festival bright.

With chatter and giggles, these oracles sing,
About wiggly fish and their glittery bling.
One tales of a crab in a shimmering gown,
Who danced through a kelp bed, then tumbled down.

Flickering lights in a jovial race,
While octopods dream of an outer space place.
With a wink and a nod, they write rhymes so strange,
Of wobbly robots and critters that change.

Gather close, as the night whispers sweet,
Inked tales of mischief, oh what a treat!
For in this black canvas, laughter ignites,
With every giggle, creating new sights.

The Celestial Hunt

Amidst the dark depths, a curious quest,
Creatures embark on a hilarious jest.
With googly eyes and fins so bright,
They search for the laughter, their guiding light.

Through coral gardens, a slippery chase,
Each twist and each turn in a merry race.
One little fish with a tickled fin,
Gets caught in the giggles, let the fun begin!

Jellyfish bounce with a glittery cheer,
As the crew of misfits draw ever near.
In a swirl of bubbles, a feast so grand,
They nibble on joy, as if it were planned.

So join in the fun of this whimsical ride,
Where laughter and bubbles forever collide.
For in the cosmic waters of endless delight,
The hunt for hilarity goes on through the night.

Sirens of the Astral Depths

In the deep, they sing so sweet,
With tentacles and rhythm, what a treat!
Their voices bubble, a wacky tune,
Dancing with planets, under the moon.

A jellyfish jam, oh what a sight,
They groove in colors, pure delight!
"Join us!" they call, with a splash and swirl,
Who knew that space had such a whirl?

Waltzing in water, a cosmic show,
Their laughter echoes as they twirl and flow.
What a party with creatures so bold,
In a universe painted in colors of gold.

With laughter and bubbles rising high,
They toast with seaweed, oh my, oh my!
In the depths where the silly do play,
Sirens of laughter lead the way!

Voyager of the Midnight Sea

Sailing on waves of midnight blue,
With fins that giggle, what a crew!
Every splash sends ripples wide,
As they prank the ship, with a silly glide.

A crab in a helmet, stars in his eyes,
Shouting funny jokes from under the skies.
"Why did the fish blush?" he quips with glee,
"Because it saw the ocean's knee!"

A starfish DJ spins a cosmic beat,
While sea cucumbers dance with their feet.
They whirl and twirl in a jelly-like spree,
Making laugh bubbles in the midnight sea.

As dawn approaches, the laughter subsides,
But memories linger like glowing tides.
With a wink and a wave, they bid adieu,
For another silly voyage, oh yes, that's due!

Celestial Creatures of the Deep

In the ocean's sky, where the funny fish fly,
With fins like feathers, they scatter and sigh.
They bounce off the bubbles, twirling in glee,
Painting galaxies in a cosmic spree.

An octopus juggles bright shining stars,
While a clownfish giggles in polka-dot bars.
"Catch me if you can!" the eels tease and flee,
A chase through the cosmos, so wild and free!

The seahorses wear their brightest tux,
With glittering ties and surprising luck.
They dance in a conga, with joy in each beat,
Creating a spectacle, oh what a treat!

From the cosmic waves where the funny ones leap,
Comes laughter and joy from the depths so deep.
With pets in their bubbles, they hitch a ride,
Celestial creatures, forever side by side!

Ink and Light

In the depths below, where the shadows play,
A creature of ink, oh what a display!
With every swirl, it paints the night,
Drawing giggles with a splash of light.

It trails its colors through the dark sea,
Tickling the fish with pure, silly glee.
"Who needs a canvas when you've got the tide?"
It winks to the stars, a clown that won't hide!

The moon shines down, a spotlight so bright,
As the ink spills stories, in sparkling flight.
"Let's create a circus!" it whispers with cheer,
With starlit balloons and laughter near.

From bubbles to giggles, they dance all night,
In a festival of colors, a truly grand sight.
With every wave, they share their delight,
In a world made of ink, shining ever so bright!

www.ingramcontent.com/pod-product-compliance
Lightning Source LLC
Chambersburg PA
CBHW060137230426
43661CB00003B/457